12/20

To R...

I hope... this beautiful Book — I bought for me (at Phipps) I think now is a good year to pass it on — to you. I know how much you and Lanie have enjoyed your beautiful nature likes/get together ((— while you have been blessed' to do together honey. Enjoy. We love ya

Amy
Chad

The Little Book of Forest Bathing

DISCOVERING THE JAPANESE ART OF SELF-CARE

Andrews McMeel
PUBLISHING®

Andrews McMeel Publishing
a division of Andrews McMeel Universal
1130 Walnut Street, Kansas City, Missouri 64106

www.andrewsmcmeel.com

First published in 2018 by Summersdale Publishers Ltd.
46 West Street,
Chichester, West Sussex
PO19 1RP, UK.

19 20 21 22 23 TEN 10 9 8 7 6 5 4 3 2 1

ISBN: 978-1-5248-5198-9

Library of Congress Control Number: 2019937380

Editor: Kevin Kotur
Art Director: Holly Swayne
Production Manager: Tamara Haus
Production Editor: Julie Railsback

ATTENTION: SCHOOLS AND BUSINESSES
Andrews McMeel books are available at quantity discounts with bulk purchase for educational, business, or sales promotional use. For information, please e-mail the Andrews McMeel Publishing Special Sales Department: specialsales@amuniversal.com

Contents

Introduction

Contrary to its name, Japanese forest bathing, or *Shinrin-yoku*, has nothing to do with wallowing in water surrounded by trees. In reality, it's the act of being among trees, absorbing the ambience of a forest. In Japan, the practice of forest bathing has existed for decades, ever since the government heavily invested in a nationwide program to promote health and well-being among its people. In recent years forest bathing has gained recognition around the world and is now enjoying a surge in popularity.

Early humans spent their first two million years of existence in the forest as hunter-gatherers, and they would spend all day out and about looking for food sources. Now, we spend much of our time inside, but we are simply not programmed for this sort of lifestyle.

Urban and suburban environments surround us with all kinds of stimuli that lead to a huge amount of stress on our minds and bodies, often resulting in negative health consequences. The relentless exposure to technology, and the expectation that we should be constantly digitally connected and available, adds further pressure.

Escaping to the outdoors is the natural antidote to our busy lives, and forest bathing offers the ideal activity to get us back to our roots and redress the balance.

FOREST BATHING
FOR
POSITIVE MENTAL HEALTH

The practice of forest bathing is scientifically proven to help us think more clearly and to improve our overall well-being. It is thought that the quiet atmosphere, beautiful scenery, and temperate climate often found in forests all contribute to this sense of wellness. But there are some more specific reasons why forest bathing is so beneficial, particularly to our mental health, which will be revealed in this chapter.

LOOK DEEP, DEEP
INTO NATURE,
AND THEN YOU
WILL UNDERSTAND
EVERYTHING BETTER.

ALBERT EINSTEIN

I firmly
believe that
nature brings
solace in
all troubles.

ANNE FRANK

Research has long shown the positive impact of nature and greenery on our overall health. The color green is associated with coolness, calm, and positivity. Placing yourself among the serenity of a sea of leaves quiets your mind and helps you find peace.

I HAVE NATURE AND ART
AND POETRY, AND IF
THAT IS NOT ENOUGH,
WHAT IS ENOUGH?

VINCENT VAN GOGH

FEEL THE
COOL
OF THE
FOREST AIR
ON YOUR
SKIN.

We need the tonic of wildness . . .
At the same time that we are
earnest to explore and learn all
things, we require that all things
be mysterious and unexplorable,
that land and sea be indefinitely
wild, unsurveyed, and unfathomed
by us because unfathomable. We
can never have enough of nature.

HENRY DAVID THOREAU

They shut the road through the woods
Seventy years ago.
Weather and rain have undone it again,
And now you would never know
There was once a road through the woods
Before they planted the trees.
It is underneath the coppice and heath,
And the thin anemones.
Only the keeper sees
That, where the ring-dove broods
And the badgers roll at ease,
There was once a road through the woods.

**RUDYARD KIPLING,
FROM "THE WAY THROUGH
THE WOODS"**

STUDIES SHOW THAT AFTER ONLY A SHORT AMOUNT OF TIME IN THE ARBOR OF A FOREST, STRESS LEVELS ARE REDUCED. WALKING AMONG TREES DECREASES THE BODY'S STRESS RESPONSE, WHICH IN TURN LOWERS YOUR LEVELS OF CORTISOL, THE STRESS HORMONE. AS A RESULT, YOU FEEL CALMER.

I am the lover of uncontained and
immortal beauty. In the wilderness,
I find something more dear and
connate than in streets or villages.
In the tranquil landscape, and
especially in the distant line of the
horizon, man beholds somewhat
as beautiful as his own nature.

RALPH WALDO EMERSON

I LONG FOR THE
COUNTRYSIDE.
THAT'S WHERE I
GET MY CALM AND
TRANQUILLITY—
FROM BEING ABLE
TO COME AND FIND
A SPOT OF GREEN.

EMILIA CLARKE

OPEN
YOUR MIND TO
POSITIVITY.

A forest environment is the perfect place for enhancing your mood and improving your self-esteem. Some traditions, such as the Chinese Taoism, teach students to meditate with trees as a way of releasing negative energies. Getting up close and personal with trees can really lift your spirits.

I CANNOT ENDURE TO
WASTE ANYTHING SO
PRECIOUS AS AUTUMNAL
SUNSHINE BY STAYING
IN THE HOUSE.

NATHANIEL HAWTHORNE

NATURE DOES
NOTHING USELESSLY.

ARISTOTLE

THE **BEST** THINGS IN LIFE ARE **SIMPLE.**

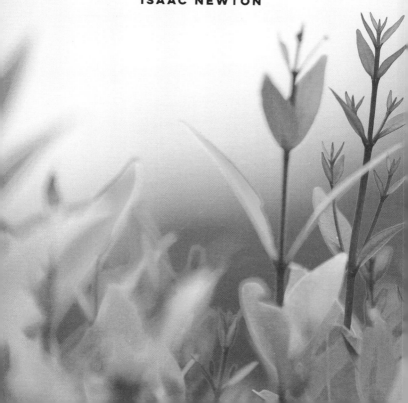

NATURE IS PLEASED
WITH SIMPLICITY.

ISAAC NEWTON

THERE'S A SUNRISE
AND A SUNSET
EVERY SINGLE
DAY, AND THEY'RE
ABSOLUTELY FREE.
DON'T MISS SO
MANY OF THEM.

Jo Walton

In our day-to-day lives, we don't usually make time to focus on all of our senses. In the forest, we can appreciate the scent of the greenery, the sounds we hear, the texture of the leaves or the bark of trees, the taste of fresh air, and the beauty by which we are surrounded.

LOOKING AT BEAUTY
IN THE WORLD IS
THE FIRST STEP OF
PURIFYING THE MIND.

AMIT RAY

I AM NO BIRD,
AND NO NET
ENSNARES ME;
I AM A FREE HUMAN
BEING WITH AN
INDEPENDENT WILL.

CHARLOTTE BRONTË

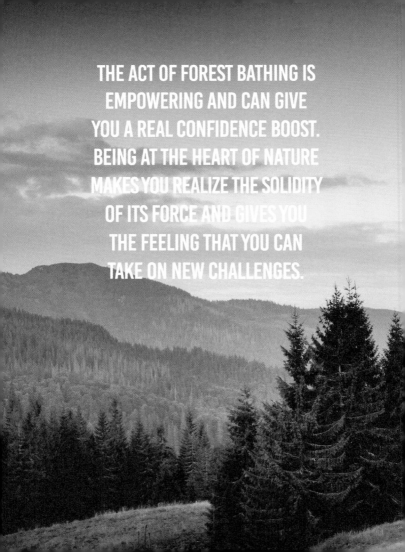

THE ACT OF FOREST BATHING IS
EMPOWERING AND CAN GIVE
YOU A REAL CONFIDENCE BOOST.
BEING AT THE HEART OF NATURE
MAKES YOU REALIZE THE SOLIDITY
OF ITS FORCE AND GIVES YOU
THE FEELING THAT YOU CAN
TAKE ON NEW CHALLENGES.

I would feel more optimistic about a bright future for man if he spent less time proving that he can outwit Nature and more time tasting her sweetness and respecting her seniority.

E. B. WHITE

FIND STRENGTH IN YOUR SURROUNDINGS.

TO SIT IN THE SHADE
ON A FINE DAY AND
LOOK UPON VERDURE
IS THE MOST PERFECT
REFRESHMENT.

JANE AUSTEN

There is another sky,
Ever serene and fair,
And there is another sunshine,
Though it be darkness there;
Never mind faded forests, Austin,
Never mind silent fields—
Here is a little forest,
Whose leaf is ever green;
Here is a brighter garden,
Where not a frost has been;
In its unfading flowers
I hear the bright bee hum:
Prithee, my brother,
Into my garden come!

**EMILY DICKINSON,
"THERE IS ANOTHER SKY"**

Studies have shown that, when measured, rates of hostility and aggression diminish among those who have been in a forest environment. Being one with nature, surrounded by a naturally beautiful ambience, promotes positivity and happiness.

NEVER BE IN A HURRY;
DO EVERYTHING
QUIETLY AND IN A
CALM SPIRIT.

FRANCIS DE SALES

FIND
PEACE.
FIND
STRENGTH.

I ONLY WENT OUT
FOR A WALK AND
FINALLY CONCLUDED
TO STAY OUT
TILL SUNDOWN,
FOR GOING OUT,
I FOUND, WAS
REALLY GOING IN.

JOHN MUIR

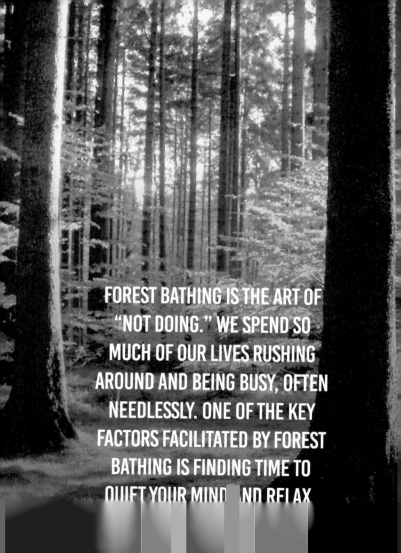

FOREST BATHING IS THE ART OF "NOT DOING." WE SPEND SO MUCH OF OUR LIVES RUSHING AROUND AND BEING BUSY, OFTEN NEEDLESSLY. ONE OF THE KEY FACTORS FACILITATED BY FOREST BATHING IS FINDING TIME TO QUIET YOUR MIND AND RELAX

OUR TASK MUST
BE TO FREE
OURSELVES . . .
BY WIDENING
OUR CIRCLE OF
COMPASSION TO
EMBRACE ALL
LIVING CREATURES
AND THE WHOLE
OF NATURE AND
ITS BEAUTY.

Albert Einstein

TODAY I CHOOSE SERENITY.

ADOPT THE PACE OF NATURE.
HER SECRET IS PATIENCE.

RALPH WALDO EMERSON

Nature allows us to tune in to our body's natural rhythms. Regular exposure to natural surroundings is proven to reduce the symptoms of mental health issues such as depression and anxiety.

I WENT TO THE
WOODS BECAUSE
I WISHED TO LIVE
DELIBERATELY, TO
FRONT ONLY THE
ESSENTIAL FACTS
OF LIFE, AND SEE
IF I COULD NOT
LEARN WHAT IT
HAD TO TEACH.

Henry David Thoreau

FOREST BATHING
FOR
POSITIVE PHYSICAL HEALTH

The practice of forest bathing is not only great for improved mental health—it has significant physical health benefits too. For instance, it can boost the immune system, lower your heart rate, and reduce blood pressure. Overall, people simply feel better when they connect with the natural environment of the forest because, as we will see, trees have natural properties that enhance our health.

Stress contributes to a range of health issues. Chronically elevated stress levels have been linked to all kinds of long-term illnesses, such as heart disease, hypertension, obesity, depression, and even cancer. Being in the naturally relaxing ambience of the forest is an instant way to de-stress.

森林浴

MISTAKES AND
PRESSURE ARE
INEVITABLE; THE
SECRET TO GETTING
PAST THEM IS
TO STAY CALM.

TRAVIS BRADBERRY

. . . Therefore am I still
A lover of the meadows and the woods
And mountains; and of all that we behold
From this green earth; of all the mighty world
Of eye, and ear—both what they half create,
And what perceive; well pleased to recognize
In nature and the language of the sense
The anchor of my purest thoughts, the nurse,
The guide, the guardian of my heart, and soul
Of all my moral being.

**WILLIAM WORDSWORTH,
FROM "TINTERN ABBEY"**

BATHE
IN THE
FOREST'S
HEALING
POWER.

Trees are nature's air filters; they help to turn carbon dioxide into oxygen via the process of photosynthesis, and they are helpful in reducing pollution by removing unwanted particles from the air. Even a single walk in the forest has significant benefits to respiration, and evidence suggests that long-term exposure to a forest environment could even reduce symptoms of respiratory illnesses such as asthma.

I felt my lungs inflate with the
onrush of scenery—air, mountains,
trees, people. I thought, "This
is what it is to be happy."

SYLVIA PLATH

THE MAN WHO IS BLIND
TO THE BEAUTIES
OF NATURE HAS
MISSED HALF THE
PLEASURE OF LIFE.

ROBERT BADEN-POWELL

FEEL EACH
BREATH FILL
YOUR BODY
WITH ENERGY.

Beyond being filters, trees provide shelter and food for many organisms. Feeling at one with a natural ecosystem, as a result of forest bathing, has a beneficial effect and promotes general wellness.

森林浴

IN ALL THINGS OF
NATURE THERE IS
SOMETHING OF
THE MARVELOUS.

ARISTOTLE

HEALTH IS THE GREATEST
GIFT, CONTENTMENT IS
THE GREATEST WEALTH.

BUDDHA

INHALE.
OBSERVE.
EXHALE.

ODORS HAVE A
POWER OF PERSUASION
STRONGER THAN
THAT OF WORDS,
APPEARANCES,
EMOTIONS, OR WILL.

PATRICK SÜSKIND

Forest bathing offers a free aromatherapy session. Natural essential oils, generally known as phytoncides, are emitted by trees to protect themselves from germs and insects. Seemingly, they also have a positive impact on humans by naturally boosting our immune system.

GOOD HEALTH AND
GOOD SENSE ARE TWO
OF LIFE'S GREATEST
BLESSINGS.

PUBLILIUS SYRUS

BE
GRATEFUL
FOR YOUR
HEALTH.

IN NATURE, NOTHING
IS PERFECT AND
EVERYTHING IS
PERFECT. TREES
CAN BE CONTORTED,
BENT IN WEIRD
WAYS, AND THEY'RE
STILL BEAUTIFUL.

ALICE WALKER

The natural quiet and cool
of the forest is a wonderful
remedy for alleviating headaches.
Part of the benefit is thought
to come from the fact that
the environment naturally
reduces eye strain.

MOVE OUTSIDE
THE TANGLE OF
FEAR-THINKING.
LIVE IN SILENCE.

Rumi

I know a bank where the wild thyme blows,
Where oxlips and the nodding violet grows,
Quite over-canopied with luscious woodbine,
With sweet musk-roses and with eglantine.

WILLIAM SHAKESPEARE,
A MIDSUMMER NIGHT'S DREAM

FIND
STILLNESS.

Exercise of any kind is good for us, and walking is one of the easiest ways for any able person to reap the benefits. The body's happy hormones, endorphins, are released when walking. Combine this with the natural feel-good factor that forests bring, and those who walk while forest bathing report feeling much better for it.

Studies have shown that forest bathing promotes sounder and more prolonged sleep. This is due to the fact that the body naturally relaxes in the forest. Our blood pressure is lowered and we are generally calmer. When your head hits the pillow after a day of forest bathing, you'll notice the positive difference in your sleep.

ESCAPE THE EVERYDAY.

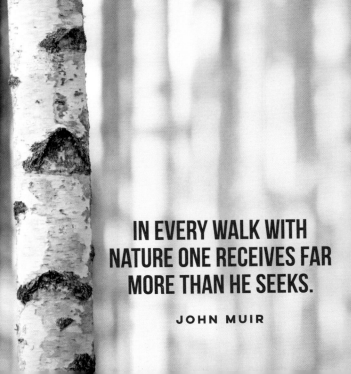

IN EVERY WALK WITH
NATURE ONE RECEIVES FAR
MORE THAN HE SEEKS.

JOHN MUIR

IF YOU WOULD
KNOW STRENGTH
AND PATIENCE,
WELCOME THE
COMPANY OF TREES.

HAL BORLAND

THE BEST CURE
FOR THE BODY IS TO
QUIET THE MIND.

NAPOLEON BONAPARTE

TRUE SOLITUDE IS A DIN
OF BIRDSONG, SEETHING
LEAVES, WHIRLING
COLORS, OR CLAMOR
OF TRACKS IN SNOW.

EDWARD HOAGLAND

When being released in healthy amounts, the stress hormone, cortisol, actually helps to regulate inflammation. However, if you are often stressed and constantly producing cortisol, the body's cells can become insensitive to its regulating effects. When this hormone is not controlled, inflammation can become chronic and lead to a variety of conditions, such as diabetes and heart disease. The calming effect of forest bathing, which brings cortisol back to a normal level, has the result of lowering our blood pressure and helps the body to reduce harmful inflammation again.

THE GOAL OF LIFE
IS TO MAKE YOUR
HEARTBEAT MATCH THE
BEAT OF THE UNIVERSE,
TO MATCH YOUR NATURE
WITH NATURE.

JOSEPH CAMPBELL

FIND CLARITY OF MIND IN SERENITY.

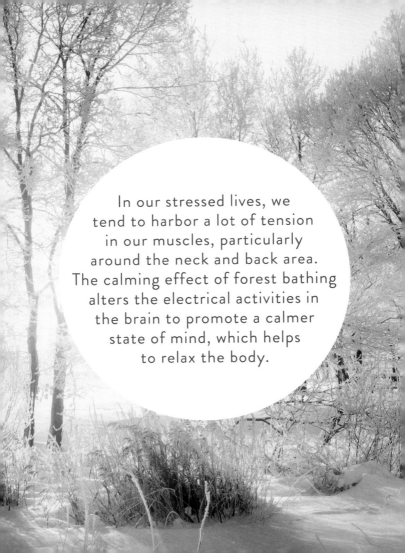

In our stressed lives, we
tend to harbor a lot of tension
in our muscles, particularly
around the neck and back area.
The calming effect of forest bathing
alters the electrical activities in
the brain to promote a calmer
state of mind, which helps
to relax the body.

GLANCE INTO
THE WORLD JUST
AS THOUGH TIME
WERE GONE:
AND EVERYTHING
CROOKED WILL
BECOME STRAIGHT
TO YOU.

Friedrich Nietzsche

There is a rapture on the lonely shore,
There is society where none intrudes,
By the deep Sea, and music in its roar:
I love not Man the less, but Nature more,
From these our interviews, in which I steal
From all I may be, or have been before,
To mingle with the Universe, and feel
What I can ne'er express, yet cannot
all conceal.

LORD BYRON, FROM
"CHILDE HAROLD'S PILGRIMAGE"

SOFTEN YOUR GAZE, RELAX YOUR BODY.

**FOR FAST-ACTING RELIEF,
TRY SLOWING DOWN.**

LILY TOMLIN

Research suggests that patients who have a wooded view from their place of recovery have much quicker healing processes. If you are feeling under the weather in any way, seek out the forest as a natural tonic.

STAND
FOR A
MOMENT
IN AWE.

WE HAVE MORE
POSSIBILITIES AVAILABLE
IN EACH MOMENT THAN
WE REALIZE.

THÍCH NHẤT HẠNH

THE BEST REMEDY
FOR THOSE WHO ARE
AFRAID, LONELY, OR
UNHAPPY IS TO GO
OUTSIDE, SOMEWHERE
WHERE THEY CAN
BE QUITE ALONE
WITH THE HEAVENS,
NATURE, AND GOD.

ANNE FRANK

THE SPIRITUAL
POWER OF
FOREST BATHING

Forests are very spiritual places and have often been the focus of myth and legend over the years. Trees are particularly significant in many traditions, as they link the sky to the earth. Whatever your beliefs, the natural peace and serenity of the forest environment offers a haven for reflection.

The beneficial effects of meditation are well known to those who practice it. Regular meditation helps reduce anxiety and anxiety-related mental health issues. Making time to stop and absorb the world around us provides a time for meditative contemplation, and what better place to try this than the peaceful ambience of the forest? The quiet calm allows you to just think about the present moment.

森林浴

THE ABILITY TO BE
IN THE PRESENT
MOMENT IS A MAJOR
COMPONENT OF
MENTAL WELLNESS.

ABRAHAM MASLOW

LET YOUR
WORRIES
MELT AWAY.

STUDY NATURE, LOVE
NATURE, STAY CLOSE
TO NATURE. IT WILL
NEVER FAIL YOU.

FRANK LLOYD WRIGHT

To see a World in a Grain of Sand
And a Heaven in a Wild Flower,
Hold Infinity in the palm of your hand
And Eternity in an hour.

**WILLIAM BLAKE, FROM
"AUGURIES OF INNOCENCE"**

Give yourself a digital detox: forest bathing is the perfect antidote to smartphones and other technology. Inspired by Buddhist practice, one of the aims of forest bathing is to connect all of your senses with nature and to interact with your environment, which you will be able to do much more easily without the distraction of the digital world.

Just living is not
enough ... one must
have sunshine, freedom,
and a little flower.

HANS CHRISTIAN ANDERSEN

Keep close to nature's heart . . .
climb a mountain or spend
a week in the woods. Wash
your spirit clean.

JOHN MUIR

NURTURING YOUR BOND WITH THE ENVIRONMENT IS AN IMPORTANT WAY OF ENHANCING YOUR UNDERSTANDING OF YOURSELF AND THE WORLD AROUND YOU. CONNECTING WITH NATURE IN A TRANQUIL PLACE HAS A POSITIVE IMPACT, AS IT HELPS US FIND A GREATER SENSE OF PEACE WITHIN OURSELVES.

FEEL THE WARMTH FROM RAYS OF SUN THAT FIND THEIR WAY THROUGH THE TREE CANOPY.

EVERY FLOWER IS A SOUL
BLOSSOMING IN NATURE.

GÉRARD DE NERVAL

CONNECT
TO NATURE.
CONNECT TO
YOURSELF.

A HUMAN BEING
IS A PART OF THE
WHOLE CALLED
BY US "UNIVERSE,"
A PART LIMITED IN
TIME AND SPACE.

ALBERT EINSTEIN

NATURE ALWAYS WEARS THE COLORS OF THE SPIRIT.

RALPH WALDO EMERSON

Immersing yourself in the depths of a forest provides a unique environment of clean air, peace and quiet, and immune-system benefits. The natural power of trees creates a healing balm for our bodies, minds, and souls; being in their presence offers a unique place for contemplation.

CALM MIND BRINGS
INNER STRENGTH AND
SELF-CONFIDENCE, SO
THAT'S VERY IMPORTANT
FOR GOOD HEALTH.

DALAI LAMA

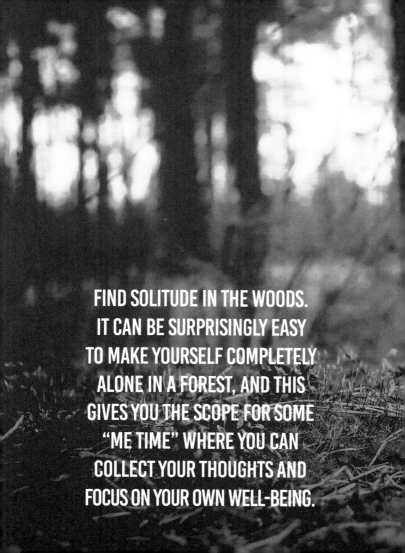

FIND SOLITUDE IN THE WOODS.
IT CAN BE SURPRISINGLY EASY
TO MAKE YOURSELF COMPLETELY
ALONE IN A FOREST, AND THIS
GIVES YOU THE SCOPE FOR SOME
"ME TIME" WHERE YOU CAN
COLLECT YOUR THOUGHTS AND
FOCUS ON YOUR OWN WELL-BEING.

PEACE IS ITS
OWN REWARD.

NELSON MANDELA

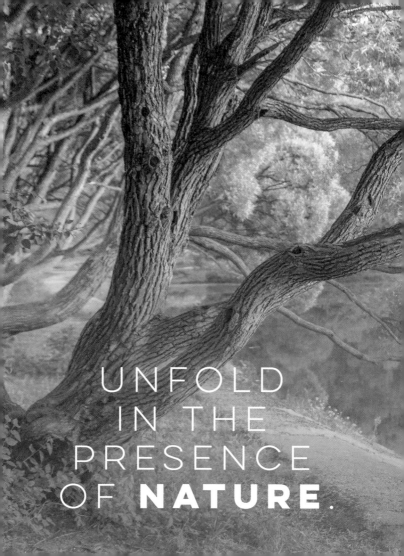

UNFOLD
IN THE
PRESENCE
OF **NATURE**.

THERE IS A CALMNESS
TO A LIFE LIVED IN
GRATITUDE, A QUIET JOY.

RALPH BLUM

THE HIGHEST
PERFECTION
OF HUMAN LIFE
CONSISTS IN THE
MIND OF MAN
BEING DETACHED
FROM CARE.

Thomas Aquinas

WHEREVER YOU **ARE,**
BE **PRESENT.**

In an age where work generally occupies more time than leisure, we often find ourselves on what can seem like a constant treadmill. Forest bathing is an ideal opportunity to help you remove yourself from the day-to-day and find your natural rhythm.

HOW TO
PRACTICE
FOREST BATHING

Now you know the science behind why forest bathing is so beneficial for mind, body, and spirit, here are some simple instructions on getting started with practicing forest bathing for yourself. There are many guided forest bathing tours available, but if you're happy to go it alone, locate a forest that is known to you, where you feel safe. If reaching a forest is too much of a challenge, find a peaceful area of open ground where there are trees, such as a municipal park. Remember to respect the forest you choose by leaving no traces of your presence and not disturbing nature.

MY SOUL CAN FIND
NO STAIRCASE
TO HEAVEN
UNLESS IT BE
THROUGH EARTH'S
LOVELINESS.

MICHELANGELO

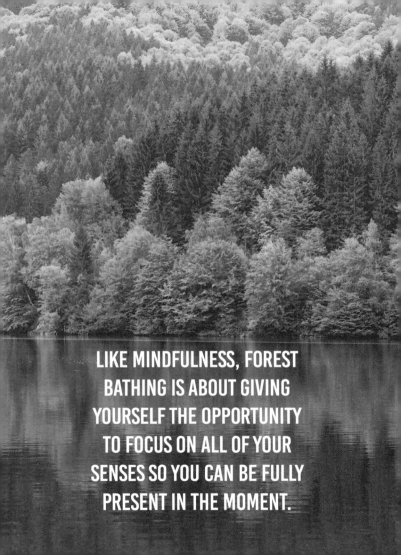

LIKE MINDFULNESS, FOREST BATHING IS ABOUT GIVING YOURSELF THE OPPORTUNITY TO FOCUS ON ALL OF YOUR SENSES SO YOU CAN BE FULLY PRESENT IN THE MOMENT.

I LIKE THIS PLACE
AND COULD WILLINGLY
WASTE MY TIME IN IT.

WILLIAM SHAKESPEARE
ON THE FOREST OF ARDEN

STOP RUSHING AROUND— STOP, PAUSE, AND START TO THROW OFF THE SHACKLES OF YOUR BUSY DAY.

When you walk in the woods, try to quiet your mind by banishing unwanted thoughts and worries. Focus instead on sounds the forest presents. It may be wind rustling through leaves, or the sound of birds calling, or it could just be the silence. Whatever it is, let your mind absorb the sounds and try to block any other thoughts.

LIVE IN EACH SEASON AS
IT PASSES; BREATHE THE
AIR...TASTE THE FRUIT,
AND RESIGN YOURSELF
TO THE INFLUENCE OF
THE EARTH.

HENRY DAVID THOREAU

WALK
MINDFULLY.

THE CLEAREST WAY
INTO THE UNIVERSE IS
THROUGH A FOREST
WILDERNESS.

JOHN MUIR

Simply breathe. Breathing exercises are in themselves hugely beneficial, but when you practice them in the clean, cool air of the forest, you double the wellness effect.

Place your feet firmly on the ground, as though you were sending down roots into the earth. Close your eyes, inhale through your nose, and send your breath deep into your belly. Slowly breathe out through your mouth without forcing your breath. Repeat at least four times— you should start to feel the calming effect immediately.

Forest meditation: find a quiet spot where you can sit comfortably, either in a clearing, on a fallen tree trunk, or simply leaning against a tree. The idea is to concentrate your attention on a specific thing and dispel all other thoughts.

To get started, you can settle your eyes on a leaf or branch that's in your field of vision or you can close your eyes. Then focus your attention on your breath and nothing else. Breathe in and out as you normally would, and notice how your body moves with each inhalation and exhalation. If this is your first time meditating, don't worry if other thoughts start to creep in—just try to pull your focus back to your breathing. Keep this going for as long as is comfortable for you, and notice how relaxed you feel afterward.

BREATHE
IN **CALM**;
BREATHE
OUT
STRESS.

FORGET NOT THAT THE EARTH DELIGHTS TO FEEL YOUR BARE FEET AND THE WINDS LONG TO PLAY WITH YOUR HAIR.

KAHLIL GIBRAN

The tree which moves some to
tears of joy is in the eyes of others
only a green thing that stands
in the way. Some see nature all
ridicule and deformity . . . and some
scarce see nature at all. But to the
eyes of the man of imagination,
nature is imagination itself.

WILLIAM BLAKE

THE MORE MAN
MEDITATES UPON
GOOD THOUGHTS,
THE BETTER WILL BE
HIS WORLD AND THE
WORLD AT LARGE.

CONFUCIUS

IS NOT THIS A TRUE
AUTUMN DAY?
JUST THE STILL
MELANCHOLY THAT I
LOVE—THAT MAKES
LIFE AND NATURE
HARMONIZE.

George Eliot

YOU ARE
PART OF
NATURE'S
GREATNESS.

To find the universal elements enough; to find the air and the water exhilarating; to be refreshed by a morning walk or an evening saunter . . . to be thrilled by the stars at night; to be elated over a bird's nest or a wildflower in spring—these are some of the rewards of the simple life.

JOHN BURROUGHS

Let yourself go and relax. Sometimes just being in a different environment can be a pick-me-up and, remember, you don't have to sit still to be peaceful. Wandering through a forest is perfect for some downtime. Open your mind to the fact that forests are proven to be naturally calming places. As you "bathe" in the forest, soak up the natural balm of the trees, and feel your blood pressure lower and your happy hormones kick in.

The poetry
of earth is
never dead.

JOHN KEATS

FIND AN OPENING IN THE TREES, TURN YOUR FACE TO THE SKY, AND FEEL THE SUN ON YOUR SKIN.

森林浴

THERE IS A
SERENE AND
SETTLED MAJESTY
TO WOODLAND
SCENERY THAT
ENTERS INTO THE
SOUL AND DELIGHTS
AND ELEVATES IT.

WASHINGTON IRVING

Forest bathing is about
getting away from it all and
connecting with nature,
so try taking a break from
technology. Leave your
gadgets at home or in the car
when you next visit the forest
and notice how liberated
you feel. Don't wander too
far if you are worried about
getting lost—the peripheries
of forests are just as calming!

If the sight of the blue skies fills you with joy, if a blade of grass springing up in the fields has power to move you, if the simple things in nature have a message you understand, rejoice, for your soul is alive.

ELEONORA DUSE

Find your voice in the forest
by chanting affirmations—
positive sentences intended
to affect and activate the
conscious and subconscious
mind. You can choose the
subject of your affirmations to
suit your needs. By repeating
them loudly and clearly, you
can change the way you think
and behave as they allow
you to focus on a goal.

REPEAT: "I AM AS GROUNDED AS THE TREES THAT SURROUND ME."

NO SPRING NOR
SUMMER BEAUTY
HATH SUCH GRACE
AS I HAVE
SEEN IN ONE
AUTUMNAL FACE.

JOHN DONNE

IN THE DEPTHS OF
WINTER, I FINALLY
LEARNED THAT WITHIN
ME THERE LAY AN
INVINCIBLE SUMMER.

ALBERT CAMUS

Her pleasure in the walk must
arise from the exercise and the
day, from the view of the last
smiles of the year upon the tawny
leaves and withered hedges, and
from repeating to herself some
few of the thousand poetical
descriptions extant of autumn.

JANE AUSTEN,
PERSUASION

Nature is a mighty force and the environment of a forest brings that home to us. Be part of something bigger by losing yourself amid towering trees, and you will get a true sense of being part of something much larger than you. This in itself is quite humbling and helps you to put your life into perspective.

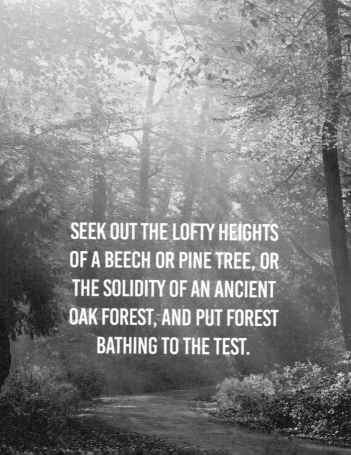

SEEK OUT THE LOFTY HEIGHTS
OF A BEECH OR PINE TREE, OR
THE SOLIDITY OF AN ANCIENT
OAK FOREST, AND PUT FOREST
BATHING TO THE TEST.

This life is yours. Take the power to choose what you want to do and do it well. Take the power to love what you want in life and love it honestly. Take the power to walk in the forest and be a part of nature. Take the power to control your own life. No one else can do it for you. Take the power to make your life happy.

SUSAN POLIS SCHUTZ

I GO TO NATURE TO
BE SOOTHED AND
HEALED, AND TO
HAVE MY SENSES
PUT IN ORDER.

JOHN BURROUGHS

Tree-hugging might take
you out of your comfort
zone but, as we know, trees
turn negative energy into
positive energy. Wrap your
arms around a trunk and
place your face against the
bark. Feel the positive energy
moving through your body
as the vibrations from the
tree course through you.

TAKE TIME OUT OF YOUR BUSY LIFE TO DO SOMETHING FOR YOURSELF.

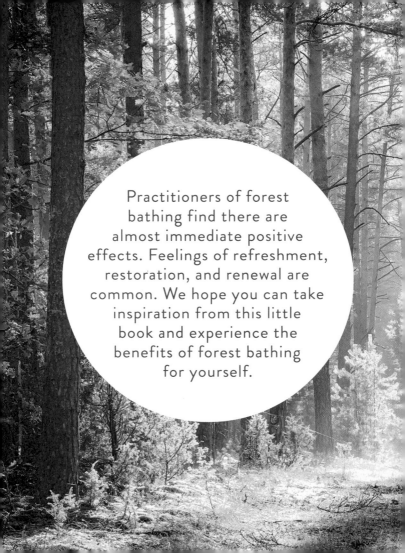

Practitioners of forest bathing find there are almost immediate positive effects. Feelings of refreshment, restoration, and renewal are common. We hope you can take inspiration from this little book and experience the benefits of forest bathing for yourself.

IMAGE CREDITS

PHOTOS